My Red Velvet Purse

A TRUE STORY

SANDRA D. RHOADS

WestBow Press books may be ordered through booksellers or by contacting:

WestBow Press
A Division of Thomas Nelson & Zondervan
1663 Liberty Drive
Bloomington, IN 47403
www.westbowpress.com
844-714-3454

Because of the dynamic nature of the Internet, any web addresses or links contained in this book may have changed since publication and may no longer be valid. The views expressed in this work are solely those of the author and do not necessarily reflect the views of the publisher, and the publisher hereby disclaims any responsibility for them.

Any people depicted in stock imagery provided by Getty Images are models, and such images are being used for illustrative purposes only.
Certain stock imagery © Getty Images.

ISBN: 978-1-6642-8350-3 (sc)
ISBN: 978-1-6642-8351-0 (hc)
ISBN: 978-1-6642-8349-7 (e)

Library of Congress Control Number: 2022920996

Print information available on the last page.

WestBow Press rev. date: 11/22/2022

WESTBOW
PRESS®
A DIVISION OF THOMAS NELSON
& ZONDERVAN

Mama, I like looking through your old photo albums. Most of the pictures in this book are in black-and-white. Didn't you have color film when you were growing up? The cars, the toys, the hairstyles, and the clothes looked so different back then. Wow! You were a little girl in some of these photographs. How old were you in this picture? Why were you all dressed up in a dress, hat, gloves, and purse? You look like you were going somewhere fancy! Where were you going?

Let me see. In 1959, I was seven years old. In those days, people got dressed up to go to church and socials, to go shopping, to go to doctor's appointments, and to go on trips by car, bus, or train. Women and girls were not allowed to wear pants to church or school when I grew up. We did not have color photos back then. In this snapshot, it was Sunday, and we had just attended church. As you can see, the picture is in black-and-white, but it was a beautiful sunny spring day. I was wearing a pretty pink gingham-print dress with white lace across the front and around the waist, a fancy white straw hat with flowers around the band and a pink ribbon that tied under my chin, white patent leather shoes, lace-edged white socks, and white gloves. And I was carrying my favorite red velvet purse.

I wonder what happened to my red velvet purse! It was shaped like a little upside-down octagonal pail with a lid that latched, and it had a narrow red handle attached on opposite sides. It was so elegantly covered in shiny red velvet with dark gold gathered lace and rhinestones around the top and bottom. The purse had a smooth, silky red lining. My aunt Dorothy gave me that red velvet purse for my birthday. Oh, how I treasured that purse! I wish I had saved it for you. I remember taking it to church on Sundays with my offering, a little Bible, and a handkerchief inside.

Mama, why was that red velvet purse so important to you?

Well, sweetheart, let me tell you the story of my red velvet purse. I grew up in Virginia on my grandparents' fifteen-acre farm. My grandparents were very godly people. My grandfather was a farmer and a deacon in the church, and my grandmother was a homemaker. In her younger years, my grandmother was a domestic worker; she cooked, cleaned, sewed, and did laundry and ironing for other people to make money. Later in her life, my grandmother became legally blind, which means she could barely see things unless they were really close to her eyes. One weekday she had an appointment with her eye doctor in Richmond, which was forty miles away. This meant I had to miss school to go with her and be her guide. The morning of her appointment, we awoke earlier than usual, ate breakfast, packed our lunch, put on our Sunday outfits, and collected our purses. My grandparents did not have a car or truck, so we walked half a mile up the road to the highway and waited for the Greyhound bus. My grandfather waved for the Greyhound bus to stop and pick us up. When we got on the bus, we made our way to the back of the bus to seats designated for black people. Although I was only nine years old, Grandma and I had traveled this route before, so I knew how to get to the eye doctor's office from the Greyhound bus station in Richmond.

Mama, why did you have to go to the back of the bus? Why couldn't you sit wherever you wanted?

Sweetheart, during the fifties and sixties in Virginia, there was a lot of racism, fear, anxiety, and segregation. Black people could not use or share the same things that white people used. We knew we could only sit in the last five rows of seats in the back of the bus. Black people were not allowed to sit and eat in restaurants or use public restrooms or drinking fountains unless they were labeled specifically for black people to use. We could only sit in the balcony in movie theaters and had to wait in line in stores until all the white customers were served first. I remember going to the doctor's office and sitting for hours in the waiting room for black people, which was the size of a walk-in closet with six straight-backed chairs. Even though we had an appointment, we had to wait until the doctor had seen all the white people first. That is why we knew we should bring lunch with us. And I had snacks in my red velvet purse too!

After Grandma's visit with the eye doctor, we went back to the Greyhound bus station to catch the last bus that had a route that went through Jetersville. By that point, it was getting dark. When we boarded the bus, my grandmother asked the bus driver to let us off at Road 642. The bus driver knew where it was and stopped the bus when we arrived there. When Grandma and I had gotten off the bus and started walking down the dark road toward home, the bus drove off. Suddenly, I remembered I had left my little red velvet purse on the seat in the bus. It probably only had about twenty-five cents in it, if that much, but I cherished that little red purse and all the things I kept in it. I became very upset. I yelled, "Grandma, my purse, my purse! I left my purse on the bus!" My red velvet purse was so pretty. I knew I would never see it again. I thought someone would probably take it for their little girl. I wept uncontrollably. Grandma tried to console me, but I was distraught.

As we walked down the dark road toward home, Grandma explained that things left on the bus would be put in the lost and found box—probably in Richmond, since that was where the bus originated. She suggested that maybe one of our relatives in Richmond could check at the bus station during the weekend. Grandma said, "In the meantime, when we get home, you go to a quiet place and pray. If it is God's will, He will get your purse back to you. Sometimes God answers differently and has something better in store."

Unless a neighbor or relative offered to give her a ride, my grandmother did not attend church much in her elderly years because of her bad eyesight. But she made sure my brother, my two sisters, and I walked the two miles every Sunday morning to attend Sunday school and church, unless the weather was too bad or the snow was too deep. She would listen to a minister on the radio or TV or would ask someone to read the Bible to her.

So, what happened with your red velvet purse, Mama? Did someone go to the bus station and get it from the lost and found? Or did someone take it?

That night, I went outside, looked up toward the dark, star-filled sky, and prayed like Grandma had suggested. I asked God to keep my purse from being stolen and to help me get my purse back. That beautiful purse was so dear to me because one of my favorite aunts had given it to me. I remembered my visits and all the wonderful times when I spent a week with her during her summer vacations. We would do gardening in her backyard, visit her friends, and play Old Maid cards, dominoes, and checkers. Many times, we would walk to the corner grocery store or catch the city bus to the five-and-dime store, and she would give me a quarter to pick out something to buy. She was an awesome cook, and she made my favorite meals (except for the one time I had to eat a liverwurst sandwich, because I didn't want to hurt her feelings).

I started to cry again. How could I tell her I lost her wonderful gift? Then I remembered what Grandma said: "Sandra, if you pray and then worry about it, you are not trusting God to answer your prayer or to take care of the situation." So, I stopped crying, looked up, and said, "Amen." Then I went back inside, ran up the stairs, and got ready for bed.

The next morning, I rode the school bus to school three miles down the highway to the wooden elementary schoolhouse for black children. The school bus dropped me and other students off and took the high school students to the high school for black students in Amelia.

The wooden elementary schoolhouse had concrete steps leading up to two covered entrances with a kitchen and workroom between the two entrances and cloakrooms inside beside the entrances. The two classrooms were divided by an accordion partition, and they accommodated first through fourth grades on one side and fifth through seventh grades on the other side. There were walls of windows on the backside of each classroom with a view of the forest. Two potbellied coal-burning stoves heated the rooms. The school did have a telephone and electricity; however, there was no indoor plumbing or indoor restrooms. The building did not have all the modern conveniences, but we had dedicated black teachers with college degrees—some had master's degrees and PhDs. The teachers treated us like we were their own children, disciplined us as such, and demanded excellence from us.

Jetersville Elementary School
1961

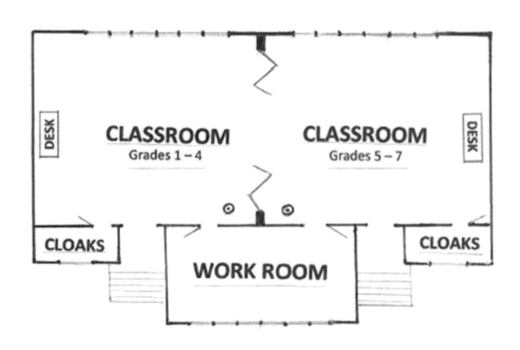

Mama, I think the lost and found box at the bus station probably had lots of things people accidentally left on buses. Did someone look in the lost and found box for your red velvet purse?

Sweetheart, that morning, my classmates and I were at recess playing in the schoolyard when a Greyhound bus stopped on the side of the highway. The white bus driver got off the bus and walked toward the school carrying a large brown paper bag. Our teacher came off the porch to meet him. My classmates and I drew close enough to hear what they were saying. The bus driver explained that a soft-spoken petite elderly lady and her little granddaughter had ridden the Greyhound bus back from Richmond to Jetersville the night before and that her granddaughter had left her purse on the bus. He said that since this was the only school for black children on the highway close to where he dropped us off, he thought this might be the school I attended. When he took the purse out of the paper bag, I ran to him, yelling, "My purse, my purse! That's my purse!" I gently took my red velvet purse, clutched it to my chest, thanked God, and thanked the driver. I was so grateful to have my beautiful purse back! My prayer had been answered!

At that moment, I knew it was a God thing. I knew I was a believer, and I knew prayer worked. That white bus driver could have thrown my little red velvet purse in the lost and found box at the bus station and forgotten about it. It was just a child's purse and of no significance to him. But he had compassion and love in his heart, and God prompted him to do a kindness. He did not care about what race I was or whether his act of kindness would have negative consequences for him from someone in his own race. He cared about showing love and helping people. That bus driver not only helped me but also made a positive impression on the teacher and students that day. I believe God used my red velvet purse to show us that love is a choice. That act of kindness showed my classmates and me that one should not judge a whole race of people by the negative or hate-filled acts of some. That bus driver had a good heart, and I think he was also a believer. I couldn't wait to get home and tell my grandmother and everyone else my prayer was answered!

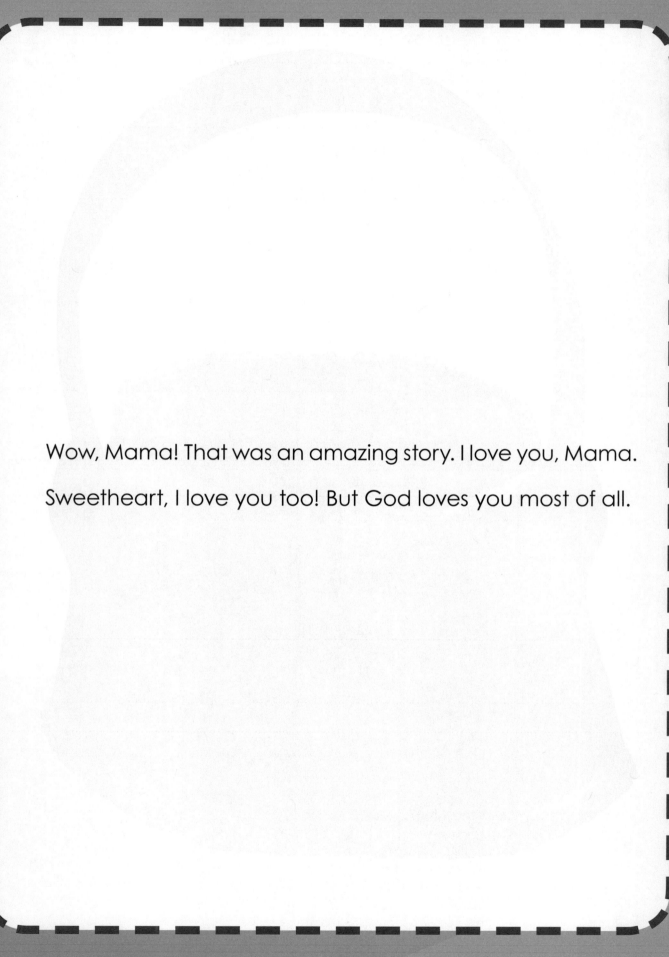

Wow, Mama! That was an amazing story. I love you, Mama.

Sweetheart, I love you too! But God loves you most of all.

Printed in the United States
by Baker & Taylor Publisher Services